Titles in this series
Don't Call Me Special - a first look at disability
I Can Be Safe - a first look at safety
I Miss You - a first look at death
Is it Right to Fight? - a first look at conflict
My Amazing Body - a first look at health and fitness
My Amazing Journey - a first look at where babies come from
My Brother, My Sister and Me - a first look at sibling rivalry
My Family's Changing - a first look at family break-up
My Friends and Me - a first look at friendship
My Parents Picked Me! - a first look at adoption
Stop Picking on Me - a first look at bullying
The Skin I'm In - a first look at racism

Text copyright © Pat Thomas 2003
Illustrations copyright © Lesley Harker 2003

Editor: Liz Gogerly
Concept design: Kate Buxton
Design: Jean Scott-Moncrieff

First published in Great Britain in 2003 by
Hodder Wayland, an imprint of Hodder Children's Books

This paperback edition published in 2004

British Library Cataloguing in Publication Data

Thomas, Pat, 1959-
A first look at racism : the skin I'm in
1. Racism – Juvenile literature
I. Title II. Harker, Lesley III. Racism
305.8
ISBN 0 7502 4261 2

Printed and bound in China by Wing King Tong

Hodder Children's Books
A division of Hodder Headline Limited
338 Euston Road
London NW1 3BH

The Skin I'm In

A FIRST LOOK AT RACISM

PAT THOMAS
ILLUSTRATED BY LESLEY HARKER

HODDER
Wayland

an imprint of Hodder Children's Books

Imagine a world where only people with red hair could go to school. Or a world where only people with brown eyes could get a job.

If we lived
in a world like
this many people
would be treated
unfairly. They would
miss out on the chance
to learn and work.

7

The way you look is decided by your family background.

Sometimes this is called your culture, or race.

Your race tells the history of your family. It is where your ancestors come from and the religion and traditions your family has followed for many years.

What about you?

What do you know about your family's history?
Does your family have any special traditions
or eat any special foods?

Our world is like a big, beautiful garden, filled with animals and plants of every colour, shape and size.

Humans come in lots of beautiful colours, shapes and sizes too. And even though we all belong to different races, we also belong to one big race. It is called the human race.

Some believe that people from their race should be treated better than people from other races. A person who thinks this way is called a racist.

Racists want to stop people of different cultures or religions living, working and learning together.

Anybody of any skin colour or background can be a racist.

Racists make it hard for us all to live together peacefully.

They are bullies who use the differences between people
as an excuse for calling names and picking fights.

Like all bullies, racists are cowards. They are afraid of anybody who looks different from them.

Have you ever been afraid of somebody that looked different from you? It happens to everyone. But most people make the effort to get to know someone before they decide about them.

Racists never do this.

They always judge others
by how they look,
and not by who
they are.

Sometimes racist behaviour is obvious. But sometimes it can be hidden in the way people treat each other or talk about each other.

You should never copy racist behaviour and, whenever you feel you can, it is good to let others know you think it is wrong.

When you are bullied by a racist you may feel as if you have done something wrong and wish you could be someone different.

It can make you feel sad and lonely and frightened.
You may not want to eat or sleep, or leave the
house or go to school.

What about you?

Have you ever been bullied because of your skin colour?
Have you ever seen anyone bullied because of this?
How did it make you feel?

You may feel that no one will understand or believe you if you tell them what is happening.

But you must never keep racist behaviour a secret.

Always tell an adult you trust about it.

The people who love you and care about you will be able to help.

Racists only see the differences between people.

But most people know that it is OK for each of us to
look and act differently, and have different beliefs.

Most people want the world to be a place where each of us gets the same opportunities to make friends and to learn and grow.

Even though we are all different, we also have many things in common that can help us get along with each other.

Remembering this is the best way to make the world a fair and a safe place for everyone to live.

HOW TO USE THIS BOOK

Racism is a complex issue that brings up a wide range of emotions in all of us. Children may be less able to express these emotions than adults. Parents and teachers can help in many ways. Here are some simple guidelines:

Children who are raised in a nurturing environment where they feel loved, supported and valued have the best chance of developing a good self-image. Those who feel good about themselves and confident of their place in the world are less likely to be fearful or mistrustful of those who are different from them. Likewise, if you are respectful of all people, your children will follow your example.

Children who are suffering racist abuse can find it as difficult to talk about as those who are suffering any other kind of abuse. This is because racist attacks can make the victim feel ashamed of who they are and lose their faith that anyone can help. A child who feels like this will need a great deal of support while they struggle to find the words to express what they are feeling.

It is common for children who suffer racist abuse to feel ashamed of their race. Young children naturally seek assimilation rather than independence. This can be frustrating for parents who wish to instil a sense of racial pride in their children. Don't force the point, instead continue to lead by example. As your child grows older the need to be like others will be replaced by pride in their own individuality.

Racism is a form of prejudice. Talk with your children about prejudice in its wider context. This includes religious and sexual prejudice, prejudice against those with disabilities and even the belief that adults are entitled to more human rights than children. Also while the common perception is that racism is directed at people of colour by white people, this is not always true. As world events have shown, racism can also exist between people of the same colour skin living in the same country.

There are many ways to teach appreciation of diversity. Try to answer all your child's questions about racial differences openly. Encourage open discussions about the ways in which we are all different and the ways in which we are all the same. In our multicultural society we mix and match many aspects of other cultures, for instance in what we eat, how we dress and the music we listen to. Point these out to your children as examples of 'common ground' with other cultures.

Schools are ideal places to help teach diversity and tolerance. Most of the time this is done indirectly, for instance by celebrating the holidays and festivals of many cultures and teaching about the traditions and foods of different cultures. Where possible teachers may wish to be more direct. Set up a 'circle time' or similar discussion groups within the class where students can talk in general about important topics such as racism.

GLOSSARY

ancestors The members of your family that were born many years before you were.

judge To form an opinion, or have your own views about somebody or something.

race Any of the major groups into which human beings can be divided. People of the same race originally came from the same part of the world and often share characteristics, such as skin colour, language or religion.

racism The belief that one's race or culture is better than another and so entitled to more rights and opportunities.

traditions Customs, celebrations or ways of doing things that are passed on year after year, through the generations.

FURTHER READING

Black is Brown is Tan
by Arnold Adoff (HarperCollins, 1992)

Black Like Kyra, White Like Me
by Judith Vigna (Albert Whitman, 1996)

Everybody Cooks Rice
by Norah Dooley (Carolrhoda Books, 1992)

How Do I Feel About: Dealing with Racism
by Jen Green (Franklin Watts, 2001)

Nappy Hair
by Carolivia Herron (Random House, 1999)

Stand Up For Your Rights
by Peace Child International
(Two-Can Publishing, 1998)

What's At Issue?
Prejudice and Differences
by Paul Wignall (Heinemann, 2000)

CONTACTS

BritKid
A website about race, racism and life as seen through the eyes of British children.

Childline
0800 1111
Helpline for children who are the victims of any kind of abuse including racial abuse.

Commission for Racial Equality (CRE)
St Dunstan's House
201-211 Borough High Street
London SE1 1GZ
020 7939 0000
Enforces the Race Relations Act which makes it unlawful to discriminate in many places including at school, at work or in shops.